MW00636258

Beach
Houses

The Deutsche Nationalbibliothek lists this publication in the
Deutsche Nationalbibliografie; detailed bibliographic data are
available in the Internet at http://dnb.dnb.de.

ISBN 978-3-03768-132-9
© 2013 by Braun Publishing AG
www.braun-publishing.ch

The work is copyright protected. Any use outside of the close boundaries of the copyright law, which has not been granted permission by
the publisher, is unauthorized and liable for prosecution. This espe-
cially applies to duplications, translations, microfilming, and any sav-
ing or processing in electronic systems.

1st edition 2013

Project coordination, layout: Michelle Galindo
Text editing: Judith Vonberg
Art direction: Michaela Prinz, Berlin

All of the information in this volume has been compiled to the best
of the editor's knowledge. It is based on the information provided to
the publisher by the architects' and designers' offices and excludes
any liability. The publisher assumes no responsibility for its accuracy
or completeness as well as copyright discrepancies and refers to the
specified sources (architects' and designers' offices). All rights to the
photographs are property of the persons / institutions stated in the
picture credits.

Michelle Galindo

Beach Houses

Living at the sea

BRAUN

Content

Preface

A house by the beach – that is the dream of many people. Whether it is a permanent abode or a simple fibro shack, the sound of the surf and the feel of sand beneath one's feet are perennially appealing. The beach is the ultimate retreat to escape the frenzied pace of our daily lives and to reconnect with the natural world. The term beach house usually brings to mind a humble wooden cottage on the shore. Today architects and designers of this field explore the conventional beach house construction, the wooden house raised up on pilings with small windows facing out to the water on inaccessible locations. The contemporary design proposals featured in this volume not only explore the material qualities of wood, but also of concrete, stone and glass; they integrate to the natural landscape and combine creative eco-conscious features and technological features into their designs with panoramic views being a crucial design element.

Moreover, open-air rooms, shady courtyards, terraces, stone, steel, glass and wood, together with exotic local materials seamlessly respond to the beach settings of these houses. The barrier between indoors and outdoors is sometimes non-existent or it is visually blurred to create a link between the two. Whether a simple dwelling on a remote island or a luxurious holiday home set in a spectacular landscape – from Uruguay to Canada, from New Zealand to Thailand – this book brings together a collection of exotic environments designed by well-known architects, such as Jackson Clements Burrows, Vértice Arquitectos, and BKK Architects, among many others creatives who draw their inspiration from the beach location, panoramic views of the landscape, and ocean breezes of the sea to orient their designs and create a unique dream home.

While many of the homes featured in the book are lavishly appointed, others simply frame the spectacular views ahead and are defined by simplicity and orientation. Some draw their inspiration from shapes whose concept behind gives character to the house. The design philosophy of others is drawn upon the natural elements of the earth in combination with different materials.

On the South Pacific Ocean on a cliff in Mantanzas, Chile, a minimalistic wooden structure rises: *D House* by Panorama / WMR Arquitectos. Two volumes intersect one another at a higher level and rotate 45 degrees in relation to the plan, allowing double heights and the organization of space in the first floor. Partly enclosed terraces allow the users to be outside the days of extreme wind. The panoramic views of the landscape, the beach and the forest in front of the ocean have been the main elements in the design of this house which sits like a jewel above the ocean.

Further up on the West Coast of the Baltic Sea, the island of Öland in Sweden lends inspiration to the design of *Villa Widlund* by Claesson Koivisto Rune Architects. The geometry of the house, a "corsetted" white concrete box provides the house with a slightly sheared wall and roof angles, giving this beach dwelling character and expression.

On the Coral Sea, *Azuris Residence* on Hamilton Island, Australia, designed by Dettorre Architects is a simple, clean space, carved out of robust masonry, ensuring longevity and low future maintenance in the sub-tropical climate. The design of the house responds to its spectacular location near the edge of the ocean and its site falling steeply away towards the water's edge on Hamilton Island. The design philosophy is based upon the emphasis on the eternal elements of sun, sea and air in combination with the materials' textural quality. The internal spaces wrap around water and courtyards, capturing not only ocean views but also inward looking private vistas.

Beach Houses features a stunning array of the most ambitious examples of residential design along the coast. From a minimalist home on a secluded island to an unusual structure high above the sea to a splendid holiday villa in an urban setting, this volume brings together a collection of remarkable houses. The contemporary beach houses featured in this volume harmoniously adapt to the surrounding landscape while embracing the seaside lifestyle with sumptuous interiors and outdoor living spaces and balancing casual-cool and opulence. They answer to today's aesthetic, functional and ecological demands, while at the same time underscoring the uniqueness of the seaside location.

from above to below: lap pool, concrete deck cantilevers over the ocean

exterior view

Al Mare

La Barra, Punta del Este, Uruguay

Architect: Estudio Martin Gomez Arquitectos
Materials: stone, concrete, wood, glass

Martin Gomez Arquitectos believe that summerhouses should transform the way their occupants live, inviting relaxation with every structural and aesthetic feature. Concrete, wood and stone were chosen as the essential materials for this house, selected for their "honesty" – their capacity to transform and be transformed – and for the lack of maintenance required to preserve them. From the outside, the residence appeals as a warmly welcoming stone dwelling that opens invitingly towards the sea. A pool integrated along the outdoor deck accompanies the entrance and brings life and color by day and night. The interior is negotiated via a magnificent staircase embedded in a stonewall and boasts stunning views at each and every opportunity.

from above to below, from left to right: interior skylight, outdoor-dining area, floating concrete staircase

from above to below, from left to right: wooden bridge,
interior opens up to wooden deck, open interior plan

from left to right: covered terrace, living room detail

view from pool

La Boyita

Punta del Este, Uruguay

Architect: Estudio Martin Gomez Arquitectos
Completion year: 2007
Materials: wood, stone, glass

The owners of this dreamy summerhouse wanted a peaceful dwelling that could help them unwind and relax during the hottest days of the year. They asked Martin Gomez Arquitectos to transform their dream into reality. Called La Boyita, the residence offers superb views over the nearby sea and the beautiful green surroundings. It consists of five areas, with the main space housing the living and dining area that opens towards the beautiful swimming pool outside. The other four quarters include the service areas and guest rooms, separated from the other spaces and allowing visitors to enjoy the feeling of staying in a deluxe hotel. This temple of stone, wood and glass really is the pinnacle of elegant comfort.

13

from above to below, from left to right: view to garden, breakfast room, detail kitchen, covered terrace

from above to below: view across from pool, living room with
double-height ceiling

from above to below: outdoor living room, terrace

from above to below, from left to right: illuminated lap pool,
dining room, view to hallway

from above to below: exterior view from pool, elevation with lateral openings

main entrance

House in Golf Beach

Cañete, Peru

Architect: riofrio+rodrigo arquitectos
Structural engineer: Jose Antonio Chavez
Completion year: 2011
Materials: concrete, veneered gray floors, glass, wood

This temporary summer home claims a magnificent spot in the coastal desert of Lima, with views towards a golf course and the ocean. A large, comfortable terrace forms the dwelling's central feature, a simple open space bordered with grass that connects the aesthetically stunning main volume with an understated pool. Large glass panels allow light to flood into the social areas on the ground floor, while the dramatic angle of the enclosed upper level both creates a striking geometric gesture echoed throughout the design and provides welcome shade on the terrace as the sun sets behind the dwelling. A neutral palette – white, gray, concrete – allows the stunning spatial and architectural features of this unique home to take center stage.

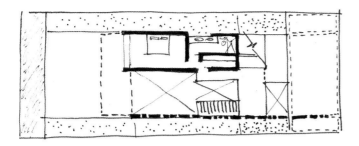

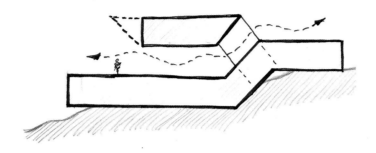

from above to below, from left to right: floor plan and diagram,
exterior view, upper terrace, interior

from above to below: view from street side, interior with
double-height ceiling

from left to right: pool with city views, staircase

general view

Beach House I-5

Cerro Azul, Lima, Peru

Architect: Vértice Arquitectos
Structural engineer: Carlos Salcedo, Jorge Haaker
Completion: 2011
Materials: concrete, wood, glass

Sited on a rocky, sandy, curving hill, Beach House I-5 has magnificent panoramic views, of the Indian Ocean to the south and of the beach to the east and north. The glorious structure projects commandingly from the rocky hillside in a series of fascinating angular protrusions, while maintaining a respectful, almost deferent relationship with the existing natural environment. Every interior space enjoys fabulous views, while the two-story living and dining area leads directly to an outdoor swimming pool and terrace, harmoniously integrating interior and exterior elements. Exposed concrete, stainless steel, tempered glass and granite stone are the dominant materials, perfectly complementing each other, the architecture and the sublime surroundings.

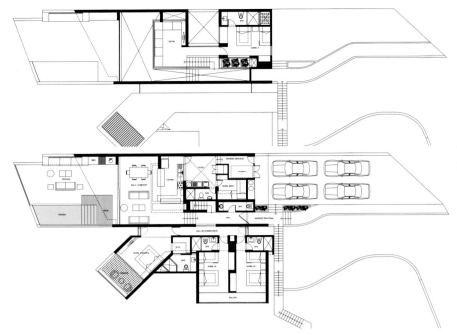

from above to below, from left to right: floor plans, staircase with panoramic window, exterior, balcony

from above to below: exterior at dusk, interior with open
beach and city views

from above to below: exterior view, interior overlooking the ocean

interior view from terrace

House PM2

Lima, Peru

Architect: Taller 33 ARQ /
Martín Dulanto
Completion year: 2011
Materials: concrete, wood, glass

The inspiration for this simple but aesthetically dynamic beach house developed out of careful analysis of the surroundings, which offer superb views from a second-floor vantage point. This led to the creation of beautiful interior patios to provide views for the first floor, which also benefits from enhanced ventilation and illumination as well as enjoying an atmosphere of cozy privacy. The communal areas – living and dining rooms, deck and pool – can be found on the second level, which opens outward to a fabulous view that can be enjoyed wholly uninterrupted by columns or opaque walls. Not only is this residence a wonderful living space, but it also invites participation in the stunning surroundings, the natural and the man-made coexisting in harmony.

from above to below, from left to right: bridge connects
interiors, outdoor dining area, concrete interiors

from above to below, from left to right: bathroom with view to garden, stairs, bedroom, floor plans

general view

ocean view from terrace

Beachfront House

Lima, Peru

Architect: Vertice Arquitectos
Completion year: 2008
Materials: wood, glass panels, concrete

Located near Lima, Peru, this contemporary house sits on a steep slope overlooking the sea and sandy shoreline of Palillos beach. To make the most of these breathtaking waterfront panoramas, the home takes shape in multiple levels, incorporating both indoor and outdoor living areas that artfully extend the home's square footage well beyond its walls. While solid wall façades flank either side of the house for purposes of privacy, its sea-side is all glass, presenting a prime vantage point to create a spectacular view.

from above to below, from left to right: interior with open
views to ocean, pool, kitchen

from above to below: exterior view from driveway, section

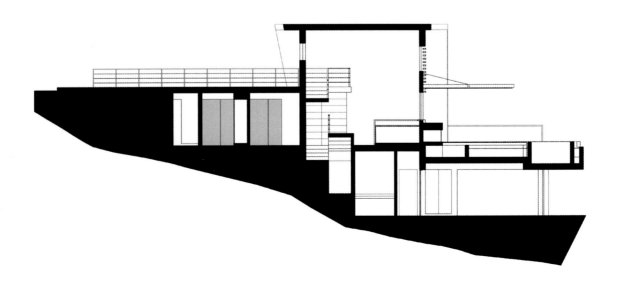

house sits partly on a concrete bed

view from the courtyard through the house to the ocean

W House

Huentelauquen, Chile

Architect: 01ARQ
Completion year: 2011
Materials: wood, concrete, glass

The owners of this rural refuge were in perfect cohesion with the architects in the design of their family home – an exercise in simplicity, austerity, practicality and pragmatism. The highly intelligent use of local materials, including impregnated pine wood and paving stones, enable the house to blend perfectly with the cactus and desert ocher tones of the landscape. Large windows create a set of transpar-

encies that allow residents to enjoy a house open to the outside, where the environment becomes a central feature of the architecture. An open-plan central interior space with bare furnishings and wooden walls painted white lends the house a summer atmosphere inviting rest and relaxation – a haven devoid of clutter and complication.

from above to below: bonfire at night, bathroom

from above to below: double-glazed windows run along the west, shore-facing
side, kitchen and dining area

from above to below: open interior with unobstructed
blending of interior and exterior boundaries, dark pine exterior

from above to below: view to surrounding landscape and beach, bedroom

from above to below, from left to right: main entrance, general
view, view to ocean from living room

from above to below, from left to right: glass walkway, living room with Chilean accents, entryway

Ranco House

Lago Ranco, Chile

Architect: elton+léniz Arquitectos Asociados
Completion year: 2010
Materials: wood, stone, glass

The Ranco House architecture integrates a bold and noble design into the existing Southern Chile landscape. A glass walkway connects two distinct sectors of the home accommodating the surrounding natural greenery. Built upon uneven terrain, the home is constructed in multiple levels which work with its geometric nature to lend the residence a contemporary aesthetic. Deep tones and colors create a camouflage with lush natural surroundings, while the interior of the home provides spacious rooms for living with rustic wood beam ceilings and native Chilean accents. The result is an amalgamation of a typical southern barn and a contemporary house, expertly integrating exterior and interior, heritage and modernity.

from above to below: view to surrounding landscape, interior
with views to surrounding

from above to below, from left to right: view from beachside, living with rustic wood beam ceilings, surrounding natural greenery, floor plans

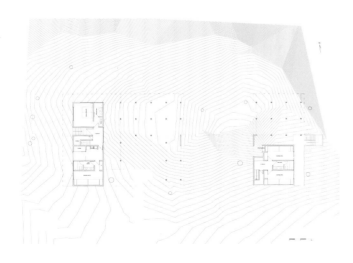

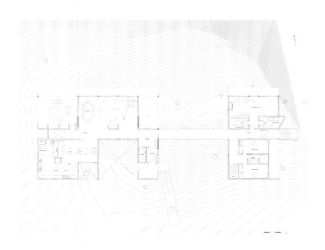

from above to below, from left to right: enclosed terrace, dining/
living room with fireplace, interior with double-height ceiling

north façade

D House

Matanzas, Chile

Architect: Panorama / WMR Arquitectos
Completion year: 2010
Materials: wood, glass, concrete

Sited on a cliff in Matanzas, Chile, D House represents a spectacular exercise in geometric design. A square volume of nine by nine square meters forms the basic structure, while a second volume, rotated 45 degrees, is intersected at a high level, generating light-filled double-height spaces. A single space is structured into a living room, dining room and kitchen, while a partly enclosed terrace allows inhabitants to enjoy being outside, while protected from strong winds. The geometric, angled design creates three distinct sectors, each oriented towards a uniquely spectacular view. A restricted palette of white walls, wood, stone and glass pays homage to both the home's natural context and the joyful simplicity of its architecture.

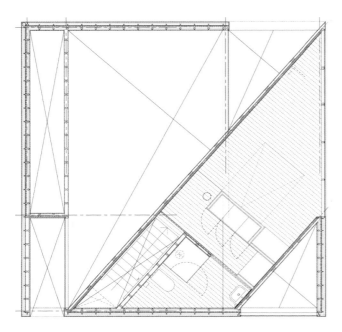

from above to below: second floor plan, interior with wooden staircase

from above to below: north enclosed terrace, house situated
on a cliff

from above to below, from left to right: rear façade, bedroom with panoramic ocean views, interior view from garden

from above to below, from left to right: wooden floors, south view, interior view from terrace, first floor plan, rear view

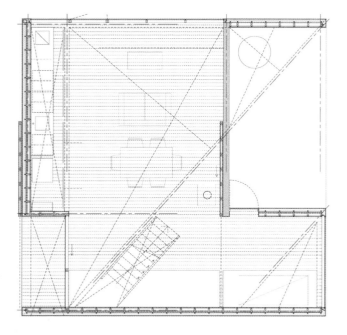

view to open interior with "muxarabi" windows filtering light

view towards house from the fjord

Pier House

Paraty, Rio de Janeiro, Brazil

Architect: Gabriel Grinspum +
Mariana Simas
Completion year: 2009
Materials: whitewashed
façades, "muxarabi", metal tile
and wood

Located in a tropical fjord accessible only by boat, the site itself is reminiscent of a lost paradise. Drawing on ancient regional construction methods and local materials, and ac-knowledging the need to preserve the dense surrounding vegetation, the architects created a sustainable, environ-mentally friendly cottage-like home that houses a boat during the week and its owners at the weekend. White-washed façades, "muxarabi", metal tile and wood mingle in a heady explosion of sophistication and simplicity. Sliding walls, wide-open windows and permeable façades allow natural lighting and ventilation. Like the boat it shelters, the Pier House symbolizes humanity and nature co-existing peacefully. In this space, worldly cares can be forgotten and the human spirit is granted the freedom to dream.

from above to below, from left to right: kitchen, detail of "muxarabi" window screens, interior, side view

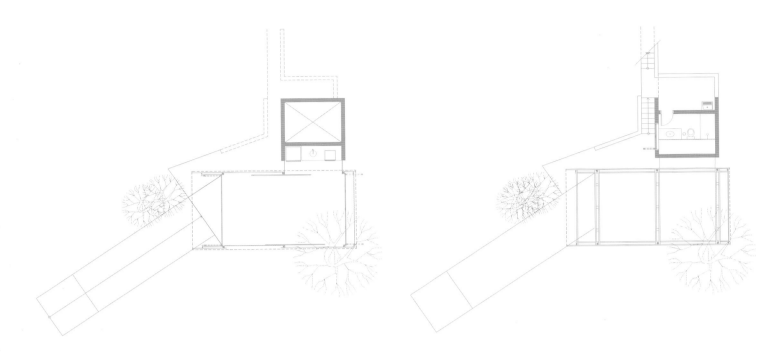

from above to below: floor plans, exterior view

from above to below, from left to right: kitchen with stonewall,
interior detail, staircase built in wood and concrete

wooden façade curtain opens up to the street

Box House

São Paulo, Brazil

Architect: Alan Chu &
Cristiano Kato
Completion year: 2008
Materials: reinforced concrete,
stone, wood, glass

The original caretaker's house on this site was a simple one-story dwelling with stonewalls and clay roof tiles. Inspired by the rustic simplicity of that residence, the architects created Box House, a two-story home formed of wood and concrete. A striking white suspended box houses the bedroom, the perfect place from which to view the continent and the São Sebastião Channel. Nestled beneath it, at street level, are the living room, kitchen and bathroom. Supported on one side by an existing retaining wall and on the other by a rough-hewn stonewall, harking back to traditional local architecture, this home is the perfect complement to its natural rocky surroundings.

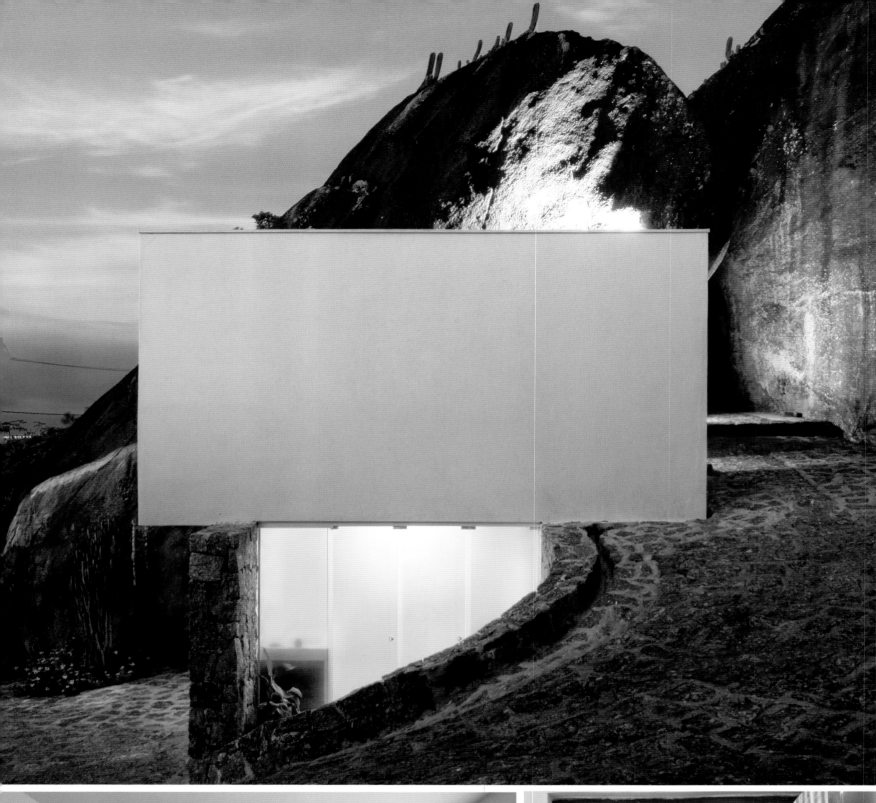

from above to below, from left to right: side view, bedroom
overlooking the ocean, window opens up to rocky site

from above to below: front closed façade, floor plans

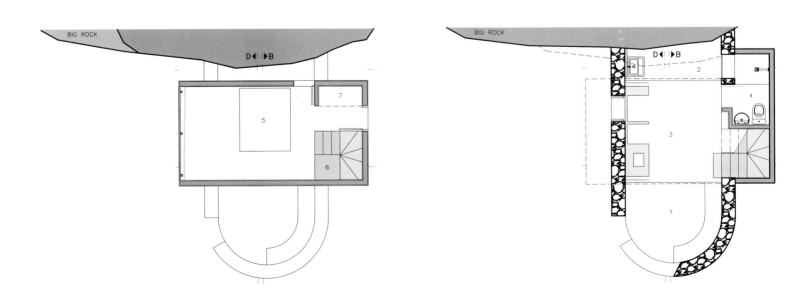

interior opens up to wooden deck

exterior view at dusk

Real del Mar House

Tijuana, Mexico

Architect: graciastudio / Jorge Gracia
Completion year: 2009
Materials: concrete, wood, glass

The steep, triangular site for this house, located within a seaside development, posed a series of challenges for the architects. A concrete wall divides the space between the main living room area and the garage space, but also cleverly ensures that the site is not overlooked by its nearby neighbors. Negotiating the sloping site resulted in an innovative three-story structure, the first two levels made of concrete and acting as a retaining wall. The smooth white façade of the upper level blends perfectly with other local residences, while retaining its architectural uniqueness. A wooden landscape area on the deck continues through the house into the backyard, merging exterior and interior in an understated architectural statement.

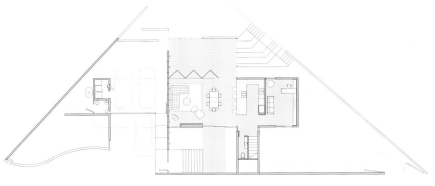

from above to below, from left to right: floor plan, main entrance gate, exposed concrete interior walls, main entrance embraces a water-still mirror and a small wooden deck

from above to below, from left to right: wooden staircase, slit
window overlooks main entrance, open interior floor plan

from above to below, from left to right: view to ocean from terrace, screen around the lanai, interior X-shaped support steel frame structure

home office/living room with open ocean views

Lavaflow 2

Kehena, Hawaii, USA

Architect: Craig Steely Architecture
Completion year: 2008
Materials: wood, steel, plexi-glass panels, glass, concrete

The Lavaflow 2 House, situated in Big Island, Hawaii, is a superb creation from Craig Steely Architecture. A cliff above the ocean offers the inhabitants both surprising panoramas of the ocean and an unusual location for engaging with nature, to be enjoyed along with all of the comforts of modern living. A cantilevered concrete slab with steel framing encloses a sun-filled glass louvered living area. The glass louvers wrap the entire building, allowing fresh air to flow through the house and inviting sunlight into every interior space. The interior combines bright and natural colors in a variety of design styles, and each corner of the house boasts a unique and eye-catching detail. At night, the house glows enchantingly like a lantern.

from above to below, from left to right: exterior view, interior clad in wood, view to kitchen

from above to below, from left to right: tub room, exterior view at
night, bedroom, floor plans, site plan

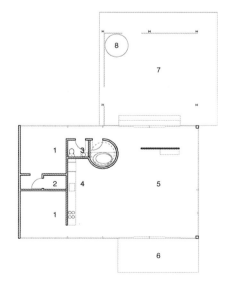

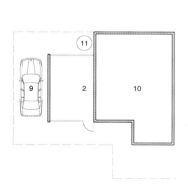

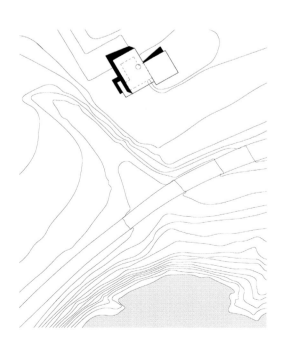

from left to right: side view, kitchen with panoramic window

view to ocean from street level

Malbaie VI Marée Basse

Cap-à-l'Aigle, La Malbaie, Quebec, Canada

Architect: MU Architecture
Project Architects: Vasco Correia & Patricia Sousa
Completion year: 2011
Materials: cedar shingles, concrete, glass panels

Located in the splendid region of Charlevoix, this exciting new residence capitalizes on an exceptional view of the St. Lawrence River, while meeting the highest standards and promoting contemporary architecture and local know-how. The house forms an angle that embraces a huge private terrace at the lower level. At first glance, the two-volume residence is both mysterious and unsettling.

Moving towards and between the two blind volumes, the visitor discovers an exceptional view from an observatory lying beneath the vast residence. The radiant concrete floor and foundation walls are left rough, accentuating the contrast with the cedar ceiling, while the ergonomic and contemporary kitchen sits in front of a large panoramic window offering stunning views over the river.

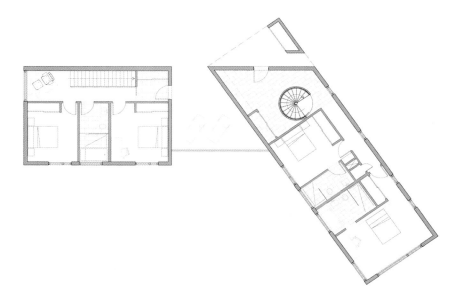

from above to below, from left to right: second floor plan, spiral staircase, living room, bedroom with extended ocean view

from above to below, from left to right: view from deck, detail
kitchen, view from bathtub

from above to below: exterior view from deck, rear view

from above to below: detail window, view from kitchen to dining room, first floor plan

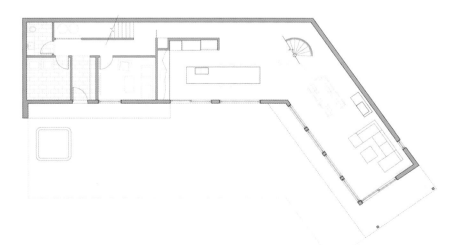

from above to below, from left to right: exterior view, panoramic
views from living room, living/dining room

side view

Malbaie V

Charlevoix, Quebec, Canada

Architect: MU Architecture
Completion year: 2010
Materials: wood, glass

The clear and simple external play of geometrical volumes forming Malbaie V seems to emerge out of the steep terrain, an impression enhanced by the green roof that integrates the house visually with its environment and acts as an insulating layer. On the ground floor, the sequence from the entrance to the main room allows for a series of unexpected discoveries through a large open-plan space.

An abundance of openings from east to west, the result of perfect analysis of solar motion and the most favorable views, provides permanent natural light as well as optimal energy efficiency. Flanked with red cedar from British Columbia on the upper volume and dyed barn wood on the lower, the house seems part of the mountain, residing in harmony with the surrounding trees.

from above to below, from left to right: volumes intersect one another, green roof, interior view from deck, interior

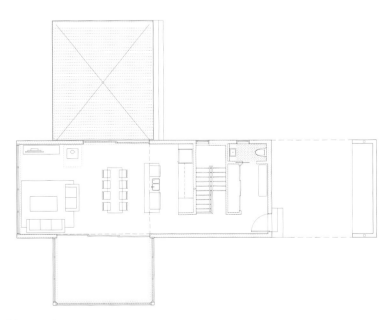

from above to below: kitchen, interior with open views to
surroundings, ground floor plan

from above to below: sun deck extends out to the ocean, front façade

top view of pool area and garden

Pure White

Almuñecar, Granada, Spain

Architect: Susana Cots
Estudi de disseny
Completion year: 2010
Materials: wood (Iroko), glass

White as the sum of all colors of light: this was the inspiration for "Pure White", a stunning architectural statement of clean lines and gleaming surfaces. Located by the sea on top of a cliff, the house is blessed with natural light which floods into the interior, a space of comfort and relaxation. The house is divided into five unique areas, including a children's wing with bold colored brushstrokes and a main suite with a dark basalt stone bathroom and distressed silver decorative frames adding minimal touches of color to the fresh white space. Large windows in the daytime zone invite the intense blue of the nearby ocean into the interior, filling it with the dazzling beauty and color of the natural environment.

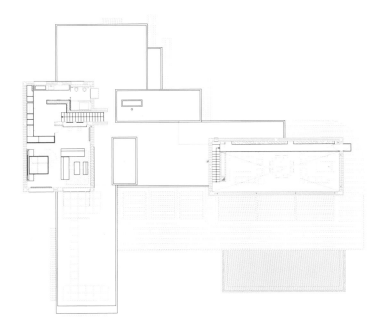

from above to below: floor plan, interior living area

from above to below: planted courtyard, outdoor dining area

from above to below, from left to right: bedroom, living room
with open fireplace, ensuite bathroom

from above to below, from left to right: living room detail, dining room, exterior view from pool, floor plans

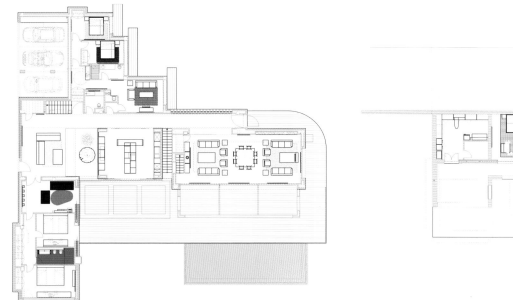

from above to below, from left to right: view to the ocean from
pool, living room, window detail

house sits atop the rocks

AIBS

Balearic Islands, Spain

Architect: Atelier d'Architecture Bruno Erpicum & Partners
Completion year: 2010
Materials: reinforced concrete, glass

The visitor to this beach house is welcomed by a rippling natural carpet that morphs seamlessly into a staircase leading down to the lower bridge, where the surrounding landscape can be enjoyed in all its beauty. A single large window frame encloses the living areas, also providing protection against the strong winds. The swimming pool lies to the side of the building beyond the terrace, complementing the surrounding natural environment. Walls and pillars, painstakingly erected on the concrete surface, support the upper floor containing the bedrooms. Perched 159 meters above sea level on a rocky cliff face, this luxury beach home is a testament to the power of the architectural imagination.

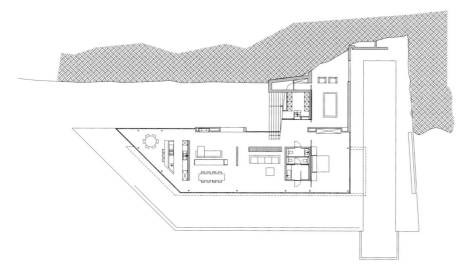

from above to below: first floor plan, dining room with ocean
views

from above to below, from left to right: breakfast room
encased with glass panels, interior staircase, courtyard

from above to below: side view, view to ocean from panoramic
window

from above to below, from left to right: open living space, bedroom, ground floor plan

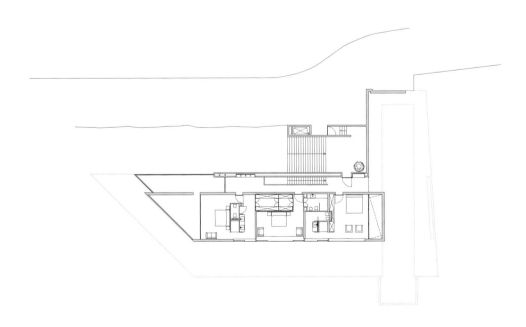

from above to below, from left to right: interior opens up to an outdoor deck, exterior seating area, view to surroundings from studio

front façade

Es Pujol de s'Era

Formentera, Spain

Architect: Marià Castelló Martínez
Completion year: 2011
Materials: rendered thermo-clay masonry, reinforced concrete, glass and iroko timber

This innovative intervention seeks refuge among existing vegetation and a fragment of dry-stone wall on the island of Formentera. The austere geometry of the home/office space harks back fondly to the architectural tradition of the island, while perfectly complementing the immediate surroundings in its dimensions and orientation. The dry-stone wall is subtly integrated into the northern elevation, bringing past and present together in a single architectural statement. An old chapel built over an underground water cistern marks out the building's longitudinal axis and forms a constant and fascinating reference of dialogue and tension, in both the exterior and the interior.

from above to below, from left to right: view from living room, bedroom, working area

from above to below, from left to right: hallway with skylight, bathroom, side view, floor plan

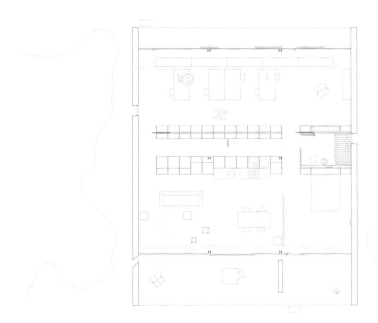

view at night

wooden deck with pool

House V

Girona, Spain

Architect: Magma
Completion year: 2011
Materials: concrete, wood, stone, glass panels

This thoughtful house plan, raised high above Costa Brava, overlooks city lights, sparkling shoreline and the distant horizon visible through expansive glazing. Minimalist interiors feature a neutral palette of white, gray and wood, infused with natural light through the massive windows. The kitchen features floor-to-ceiling sliding glass doors overlooking an outdoor dining area, set on a luscious wood deck with a pool, which illuminates at night and is enclosed in an open frame structure that can be covered with shades. Unique about this hillside home, it functions as a single-family house but can easily be divided into three separate homes, all sharing the stunning outdoor entertaining areas.

from above to below, from left to right: dining area, living room with ocean views, kitchen, view from driveway

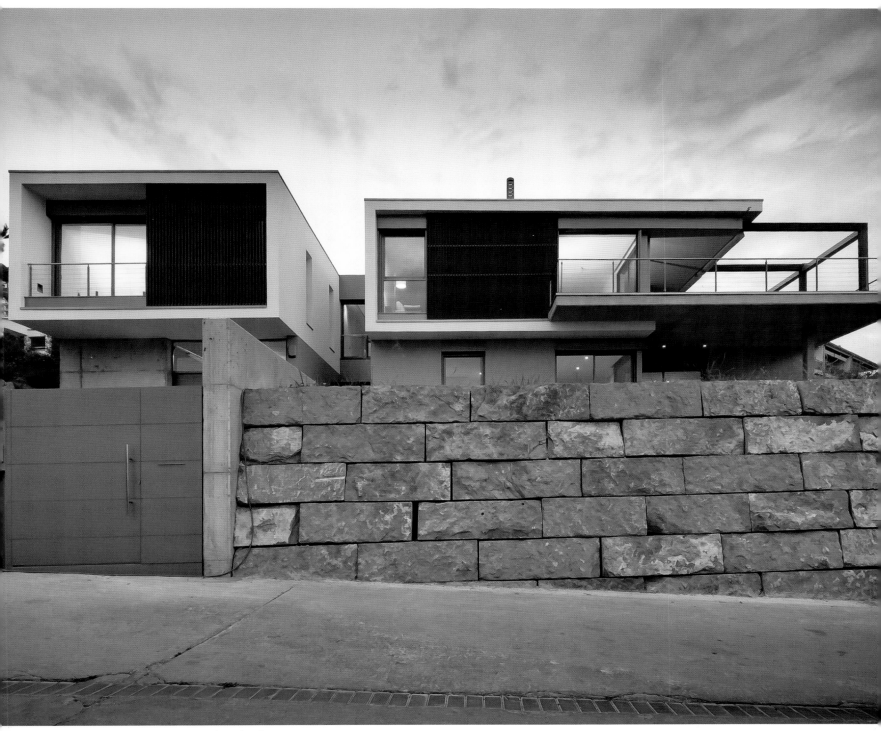

from above to below: floor plans, front façades

from left to right: ocean view from pool, outdoor shower

exterior view from pool

Dupli Dos Residence

Ibiza, Spain

Architect: Juma Architects
Collaborating architects: Minimum Arquitectura
Completion year: 2012
Materials: wood, glass panels, concrete

Located in Ibiza, Spain, the Dupli Dos residence features jaw-dropping views of the Mediterranean. Beginning as two separate duplexes merged together, this contemporary home with clean lines and neutral color tones boasts four bedrooms, four bathrooms and two pools. Inside, a floating bed of spacious white rooms are accented with bold textures and rustic metal and wood, while a refreshing outdoor pool and multilevel deck create a tranquil atmosphere ideal for enjoying the salty sea breeze. The first floor is defined by its extensive and extravagant use of glass in the form of floor-to-ceiling windows. Styled with decor and furnishings proclaiming that "less is more", this is one gorgeous house that matches the grandeur of the views it offers with the elegance of its interiors.

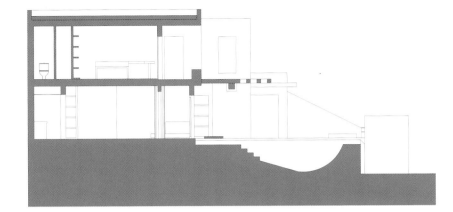

from above to below: section, outdoor dining area

from above to below, from left to right: living room, interior
detail, swimming pool

from above to below, from left to right: view to bathroom from
living room, living room, interior view from swimming pool

from above to below, from left to right: view to fireplace, detail staircase, floor plans

from above to below, from left to right: infinity pool floats over the ocean, kitchen/dining room, courtyard

exterior view from pool

Tamarit House

Tarragona, Spain

Architect: Xavier Vendrell
Studio
Completion year: 2003
Materials: concrete, wood, glass

Located on the seafront, surrounded by pine trees and lapped by the warm waters of the Mediterranean Sea, Tamarit House takes full advantage of its glorious surroundings. The first floor's children's and guests' bedrooms share a wonderfully open central common area with access to a terrace, while the top floor boasts extensive views from a large space perfect for socializing or relaxing. The design also takes full advantage of local architectural tradition, merging these concepts with the latest advances in energy sources and home automation, generating a structure that perfectly integrates past, present and future. Sliding windows can be fully opened and integrated into the walls, allowing the warm breeze to drift around the beautiful interior.

from above to below, from left to right: living room with hanging fire orb, bedroom, bathroom

from above to below, from left to right: kitchen, interior, view to infinity pool from garden, floor plan

from above to below: houses terraced down to ocean, view from
pool area

exterior view from pool

Summer Houses

Paros, Cyclades, Greece

Architect: React Architects
Completion year: 2010
Materials: concrete, glass panels

Overlooking the sea and the neighboring island of Antiparos, each of these two summer homes is centered around a courtyard and swimming pool, ideal outdoor spaces for soaking up the spectacular views. White façades reflect both the brilliant sunlight and traditional architecture, while the intense shadows created by the structure's geometric forms generate breathtaking visual impact.

Wide staircases lead to large viewing plateaus – just one example of indoor and outdoor spaces merging, their boundaries dissolving. Mulberry trees and other vegetation have been introduced on roofs and in courtyards, softening the angular shapes and monotone walls of the residence. It is hard to imagine a beach house more perfectly suited to its environment.

from above to below: floor plan, terrace bird's-eye view

from above to below: private terrace, planted exterior

view from the roof to extended deck

house is surrounded by gigantic rocks and low vegetation

Villa Mecklin

Velkua, Naantali, Finland

Architect: Huttunen–Lipasti–
Pakkanen Architects
Completion year: 2008
Materials: wood, glass

Surrounded by vegetation, Villa Mecklin nestles into a small depression in the rocky landscape, quite at home in the middle of a narrow zone of trees. Constructed from untreated wood, which will weather attractively over time, the residence rests gently on the ground as a passive and welcome addition to the wilderness, a manmade counterpart to the natural context. Inside, a minimal, open-plan living, kitchen and dining area opens onto an extended outdoor deck in a further affirmation of the harmonious relationship between interior and exterior, the architectural and the natural. Evenings spent in this villa offer a glorious sunset enjoyed around an open fire in the sunken pit on the outdoor deck.

111

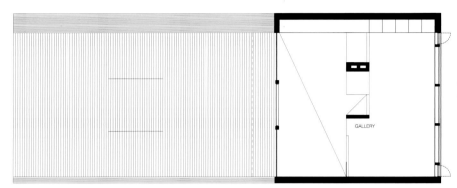

from above to below: gallery floor plan, view to sauna from the terrace

from above to below, from left to right: sauna rear view,
sunken open fire pit, looking towards the bedroom gallery

from above to below, from left to right: terrace view opening
to the archipelago, bedroom, sauna dressing area

from above to below: dining room, view across the ocean from entrance, ground floor plan

115

from above to below: street façade with minimal window openings, glass façade oriented towards the view

wrap-around patio

Summer Retreat

Fuglevik, Norway

Architect: Reiulf Ramstad Arkitekter
Completion year: 2011
Materials: wood, glass

Summer Retreat is a residence in Fuglevik, Norway designed by Oslo-based practice Reiulf Ramstad Arkitekter. The structure is clad in wooden planks and its solid entry façade creates a mono-view, directing attention towards the landscape in one direction to produce a heightened connection with the ocean. Minimal penetrations and windows allow sufficient circulation of air and light through the interior, while the rear of the home opens as a continuous glass façade. The uniform wooden interior unfolds with a partially screened veranda which frames an outdoor seating area with views towards the water.

from above to below: steps leading to entrance, building is
lifted off the ground

from above to below, from left to right: reflection within glass façade, view from veranda, front door, floor plan

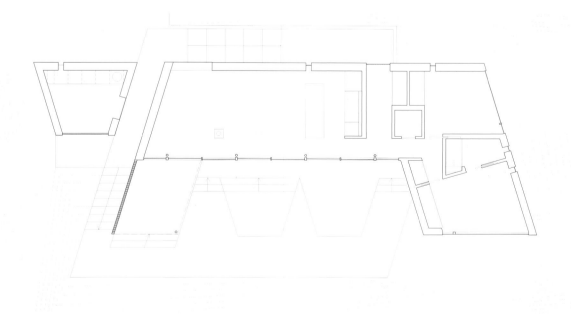

from left to right: living room, view to living room and across to beach from stairs

house with slanted roofs and walls

Villa Widlund

Öland, Sweden

Architect: Claesson Koivisto Rune
Completion year: 2011
Materials: precast concrete, wood, glass

Villa Widlund is a funnel of light, space and sea views. The white concrete box is "corsetted" in the middle, creating an aesthetically intriguing sheared wall and unusual roof angles. Lending the house a unique character, this feature also functions to separate the private rear bedroom section and the communal front area. Precast concrete was the ideal material for achieving both ultimate precision in manufacturing tolerance and a wonderful glow, emitted from every inch of the solid white surface. The joints between the concrete elements were carefully designed and positioned to become part of the building's geometry and expression. Indeed, this structure is the ultimate in functionality, simplicity and architectural cohesion.

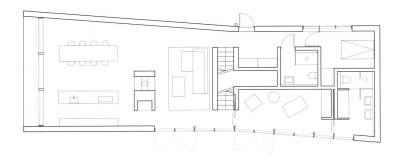

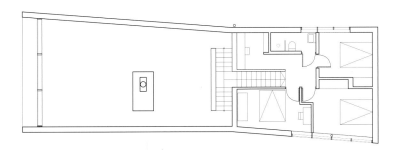

from above to below: floor plans, living room with
open beach view

from above to below, from left to right: rear façade, detail
façade, exterior view from beachside

from above to below, from left to right: wrap-around deck,
office in mezzanine level, bedroom with view to interior courtyard

from above to below: kitchen overlooking beach, wooden staircase, section

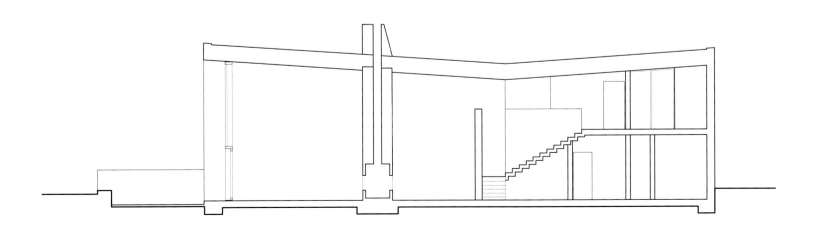

extended views from living room

view from beachside

Star House

Bnaider, Kuwait

Architect: AGI architects
Completion year: 2011
Materials: concrete, wood, glass panels

Nestled into the landscape, Star House merges seamlessly with the natural topography of the Kuwait coastline, slowly revealing itself to the curious visitor approaching from the desert. On entering the residence, the visitor is treated to tantalizing glimpses of the sea while descending into the public area of the chalet. On this lower level, the house extends into the surrounding landscape and the sea, accentuated by a stunning infinity pool in the garden. Private areas are concealed from visitors by a bamboo wall, while a three-way stair at the center perfectly organizes the various flows of family, friends and guests. Floor-to-ceiling windows on the side of the house facing the beach allow panoramic views towards the sea – a fabulous vista.

127

from above to below, from left to right: floor plan, interior detail, exterior at night

from above to below: courtyard, front façade

from above to below: exterior view from pool area, living room

from above to below: detail staircase, illuminated stairs, section

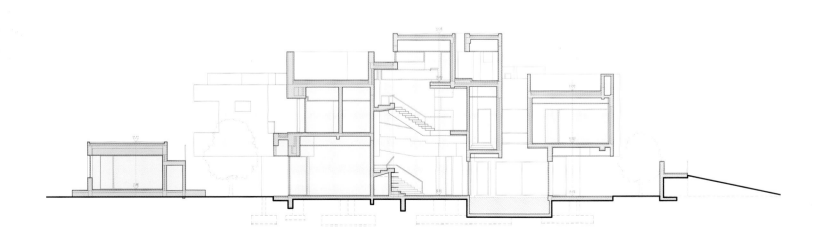

from above to below: view from garden, front façade

ocean view from plunge pool

S Cube Chalet

Kuwait City, Kuwait

Architect: AGI architects
Completion year: 2011
Materials: concrete, wood, glass panels

A beach house like no other, S Cube Chalet is designed to perfectly accommodate three families, each enjoying complete independence and privacy. Each of the three houses also boasts an individual outdoor area open to the sky and extensive sea views. The design called for a duplicated program and is structured around the outdoor spaces on the ground floor and a roof terrace with spectacular views on top of the third house. The outdoor spaces capture the prevailing winds and enhance the circulation of air within the courtyards, while exposure to the sun on the southern façade is carefully controlled to keep the interior pleasantly cool. These intertwined houses represent the epitome of functionality and aesthetic success.

from above to below, from left to right: living room, hallway, exterior view to circulation shaft, exterior view at night

from above to below: driveway, dining room

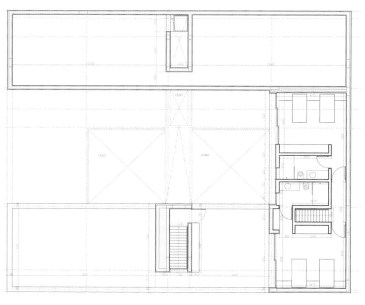
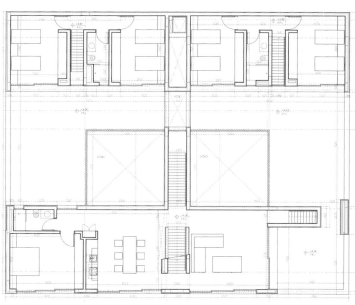

from above to below: outdoor living area, floor plans

from above to below: aerial view, illuminated exterior, ocean view from covered terrace

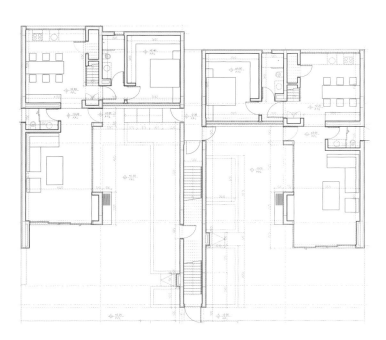

137

from above to below: view from pool, outdoor living area

terrace overlooking the ocean

Villa of a Million Stars

Koh Tao, Thailand

Architect: Saenz de Santamaria Designs
Completion year: 2011
Materials: wood, stone, glass, concrete

With a name to inspire the most wonderful of dreams, the Villa of a Million Stars is a trendy refuge in which to relax, tune in and turn off. Perched on a hillside on the tiny island of Koh Tao, Thailand, it offers spectacular views of Sairee town and the rolling waves of the open ocean. This stunning view is matched by the equally stunning designer interiors. Stylish bedrooms and bathrooms, a private swimming pool, vast open-plan kitchen, dining and living areas, and dappled terraces await the world-weary traveler, who finds peace and tranquility in these elegant surroundings. Surrounded by tropical vegetation, frangipani gardens and natural boulders, the villa is seamlessly integrated into its landscape and offers the possibility of a new kind of relationship between man and the natural world.

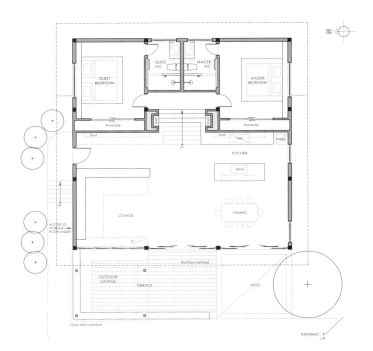

from above to below: floor plan, open-plan interior

from above to below, from left to right: pool at night, bedroom,
dining room

from above to below, from left to right: wooden deck, interior pond opens up to ocean, living room

bird's-eye view to pool

Villa Mayavee

Phuket, Thailand

Architect: Tierra Design
Completion year: 2009
Materials: concrete, glass, stone, wood

Located within the dramatic, undulating terrain of Phuket, far removed from the tourist areas, Villa Mayavee represents the ultimate tranquil living experience. While commanding panoramic views of the Andaman Sea and surrounding hills, the site also belongs to a lush tropical landscape sensitively established by the owner. Unique spatial experiences are generated by the Z-shaped structure at the center of the site, while cobbled walls meander through it. Inspired by traditional Thai architecture, the villa consists of separate pavilions but boasts an overall cohesion. The union of tradition and modernity is also manifest in the combination of stone and glass as primary materials. Indeed, this dwelling is a masterpiece of synthesis — past and present, seclusion and openness, manmade and natural coexist in perfect harmony.

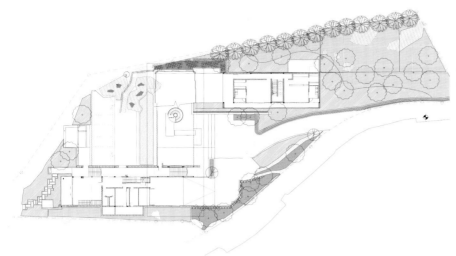

from above to below, from left to right: floor plan, bathroom, interior, dining room with view to surroundings

from above to below, from left to right: pool appears to float above
the ocean, living room, bedroom with panoramic ocean view

from above to below: front façade, dining room

interior opens onto the ocean

C House

Punta Fuego, Batangas, Philippines

Architect: Archipelago Design Works
Completion year: 2007
Materials: wood, glass panels, concrete

Architect Chut Cuerva of Archipelago Design Works has recently completed work on a stunning home for himself and his family, designed in concert with Tisha de Borja. The C House is a bright, airy and open home with a strong, modern street presence and an interior focus on the sea beyond. Aside from a few natural wood accents, the home is largely white – allowing the furnishings and the inhabitants themselves to become the home's primary colors. The rear of the home opens to a large furnished patio with wide and open views of the coastal Batangas environment. The sea stretches to the horizon, dotted with rising rocks and mountainous islands, providing a picturesque backdrop to life in the C House.

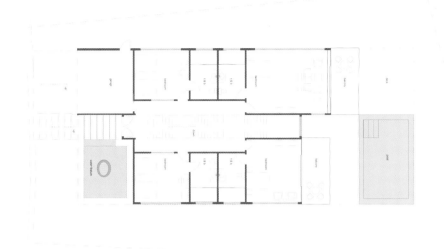

from above to below, from left to right: floor plan, main entrance, interior staircase

from above to below, from left to right: detail living room,
view to ocean from staircase, living room

from left to right: side view, ocean view from living room

front façade

Beach House

Shima, Mie, Japan

Architect: Yamamori Architect & Associates
Completion year: 2010
Materials: exposed concrete, corten steel plate, Japanese cypress flooring

Sited in Shima-city, this dazzling residence with panoramic views of the beach blends beautifully into the natural coastal environment. A series of dynamic, angular forms are brought together in harmony, enabling the structure to complement both the natural and the man-made contexts that surround it. The surprising elevational variations between ground, structure and interior, and the complex layering of spaces within the dwelling, where the main social programs are located on the highest level with un-interrupted views across the tranquil bay, invite the curious visitor to explore the fascinating architecture. A glazed wall draws natural light and scenery inward, merging the geometric structure perfectly with its coastal context.

from above to below, from left to right: detail interior lighting, interior with slanted ceiling, view to dining room from mezzanine floor, exterior stairs

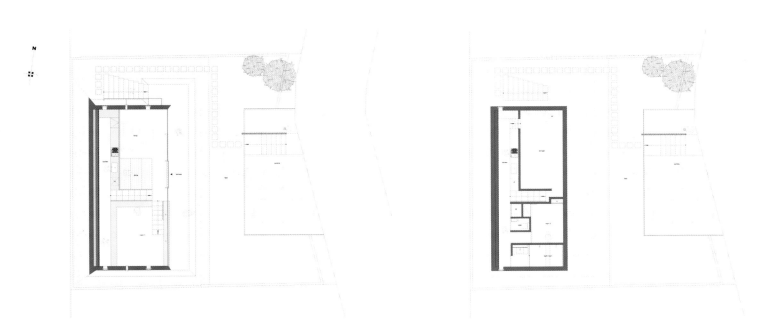

from above to below: floor plans, ocean view from kitchen

street façade at dusk

stepped terrace with integrated seating

Wind-dyed House

Yokosuka Kanagawa, Japan

Architect: Kazuhiko Kishimoto / acaa
Structural engineer: Takahiro Suwabe
Completion year: 2011
Materials: wood, polycarbonate panels, concrete, glass

The architects sought to minimize the impact of this residence on its environment by preventing its walls from becoming surfaces that would obstruct or impede movement and sight. Glass and screens positioned along the enclosed perimeter of the house lend a transparency to the second floor, while slender, deep-set eaves cast shadows on the building's façade. The first story features a stone floor and concrete walls finished with plaster, while Japanese paper screens fitted inside the glass reflect the shadows of plants and trees. An open-plan living space can be found on the second floor. A series of wide eaves stand between the outside of the house and the interior, which is articulated into smaller sections by a row of iron pillars arranged in a dense formation.

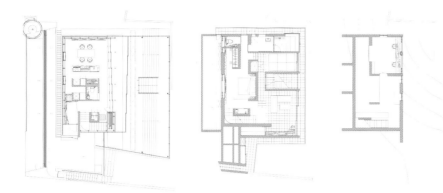

from above to below: floor plans, living room

from above to below, from left to right: dining area opens to
terrace, engawa, interior and exterior blend together

from left to right: interior view from terrace, detail bathroom

view from garden

Pohutukawa Beach House

Auckland, New Zealand

Architect: Herbst Architects
Completion year: 2012
Materials: wood, glass panels

Initially posing a challenge for the architects, the existing Pohutukawa trees on the site of this beach house soon became the inspiration for its design. Working round the trees, they decided to house the private and public living areas inside two towers, their façades covered with pieces of wood of varying sizes and shapes, painted dark brown to create a natural bark-like effect. Large corner-cut windows flood the bedrooms with light and expose natural light colored timber to the exterior, enhancing the impression of these towers as freshly sawn tree stumps, part of the natural world. Continuing the theme, wooden porches wrap around the entire façade, topped with a frayed edge roof, which – just like a leaf canopy – filters dappled light into the residence.

from above to below, from left to right: floor plans, deck,
reading area, bedroom

from above to below, from left to right: aerial view of living
room, living room, interior with double-height ceiling

from above to below, from left to right: general view, interior with
fireplace, dining room

view from beachside

Drift Bay House

Queenstown, New Zealand

Architect: Kerr Ritchie Architects
Completion year: 2007
Materials: concrete, steel, wood, glass

This family home was designed as a single fluid form that reclines into the sloping landscape on the edge of Lake Wakatipu. The long black form shifts and expands to suit the sun, the occupants' needs and the site. The roof and walls of the house are clad in black steel and timber weatherboards. The entry is through a hole punched in the middle creating a courtyard. This allows visitors to enter either the family home to the north or the studio/guest wing to the south. The interior is intended to have the resilience of an institutional building. Space shifts, as well as form, up and down to create spaces that move from snug to lofty and back again.

164   from above to below: detail façade, aerial view

from above to below, from left to right: kitchen, main entrance, floor plans

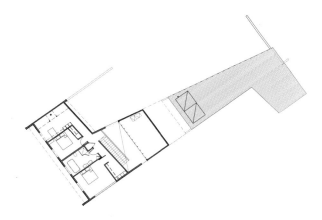
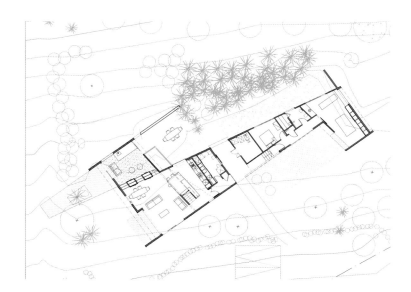

from above to below: pool looking north-east over beach, view from pool area

entranceway

Okitu House

Tatapouri Point, New Zealand

Architect: Bossley Architects
Interior designer: Karen Ngan Kee
Completion year: 2003
Materials: concrete, wood, glass

This house by one of New Zealand's foremost architects is located on a coastal hillside just north of Gisborne with spectacular views. The single-story house clings to the ground as it steps down then opens out towards the sea to become a striking grandstand for viewing. Sheltered outdoor areas, created by the unusual T-shaped plan, offer welcome protection from strong winds, while a large, comfortable terrace is located at the north end of the house to extend the building into the landscape, creating a dynamic and visually exciting relationship between the two. Exposed steel, concrete and aluminum are complemented by timber and glass to generate a structure that is wonderfully involved in both the man-made and the natural world.

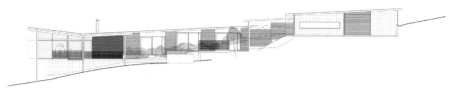

from above to below: east elevation, looking from the deck towards interior

from above to below: south façade, dining/living area with
ocean views

from above to below, from left to right: bedroom looking out
to the sea, east view, kitchen/dining area

from above to below: courtyard, floor plans

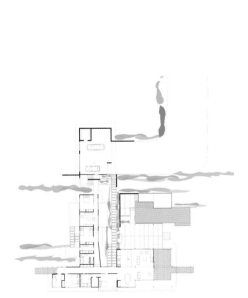

from above to below, from left to right: view to interior from terrace, kitchen

view to ocean from terrace

Bondi House

Bondi Beach, Australia

Architect: Redgen Mathieson
Collaborating architect: David Katon
Completion year: 2011
Materials: marble, glass, wood

Located on Sydney's Bondi Beach, this sublime four-level house occupies a narrow infill site and offers spectacular views towards the beach. The ground level accommodates the entry hall and two bedrooms, one opening onto a courtyard with a cut-out that perfectly frames the sweep of the beach, the other onto a beautiful courtyard garden planted with bamboo. A majestic marble clad stairway leads to an open-plan living level with a central kitchen of rich bronze and dark brown stone. White terrazzo, Calacatta marble, American walnut timber and dark bronze combine to create a luxurious interior palette that is complemented by a dramatic glass and white marble façade.

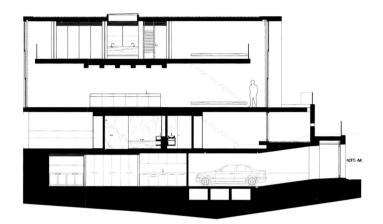

from above to below, from left to right: section, staircase, dressing room and spacious marble ensuite, Calacatta marble interior

from above to below, from left to right: view down to pool,
exterior view, living room opens up to the ocean

from above to below, from left to right: marble ensuite,
bedroom with ocean views, front façade at night

from above to below, from left to right: master bedroom, floor plans

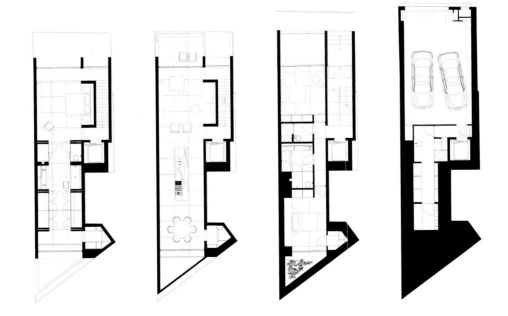

from above to below: exterior view from terrace, exterior view
from beachside

dining room with open ocean views

Scapehouse

Cape Liptrap, Victoria, Australia

Architect: Andrew Simpson Architects
Structural Engineer: Adams Consulting Engineers
Completion year: 2009
Materials: wood, steel, concrete, glass panels

This project for a family coastal residence is located on a stunning isolated site in eastern Victoria, with sublime panoramic views. It represents a fascinating investigation of how an idealized conception of a "house" is transformed by its specific context and use – in this case; an idealized profile of a gabled house has been incorporated and subverted to accommodate spectacular views of the landscape from the two wings. These arms of the building create a sheltered area to the north side, providing welcome relief from the harsh prevailing winds. The interior space boasts impressive flexibility of use and can provide accommodation for a single guest or a large extended family enjoying a relaxing holiday.

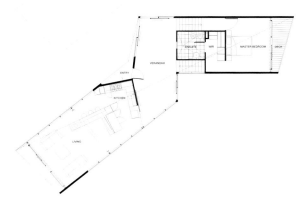

from above to below, from left to right: floor plans, living room, detail exterior façade

from above to below: general view, interior

from above to below, from left to right: house integrates with its
surrounding bushlands, aerial view, open pavilion

views across the Coral Sea

Azuris Residence

Hamilton Island, Australia

Architect: Renato D'ettorre
Architects
Completion year: 2009
Materials: concrete, glass, stone, wood

Azuris Residence on Hamilton Island was built by Dettorre Architects and comprises a series of simple, clean spaces carved out of robust masonry, generating a sense of both weight and lightness, and ensuring longevity and low maintenance in the sub-tropical climate. The design of the house responds perfectly to its spectacular location near the edge of the ocean and emerged from a philosophy based on the eternal elements of sun, sea and air. Materials with fascinating textural qualities were introduced to render the dwelling almost indistinguishable from its surroundings. Internal spaces wrap themselves around water and courtyards, capturing not only ocean views but also inward looking private vistas.

from above to below, from left to right: site plan, pool hangs over living room, courtyard, bedroom with open floor plan

from above to below: stonewalls surround the house,
bedroom opens up to pool and views across the ocean

from above to below, from left to right: floating stone deck with
views across ocean, house wraps around a pool and ponds, sliding
glass walls open up to corridor

from above to below, from left to right: exterior stairs step down to the house, bathroom with ocean views, bedroom opens up to pool, floor plans

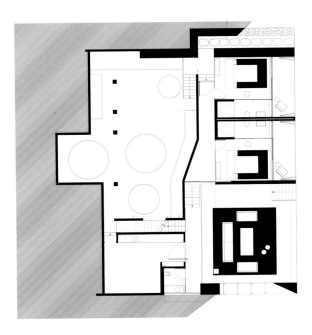
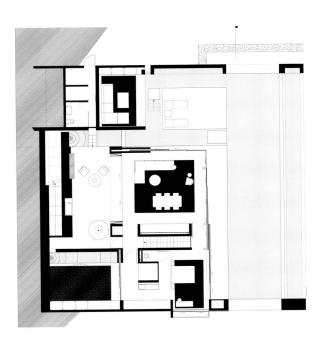

interior view from wrap-around terrace

exterior view from beachside

NSW North Coast House

New South Wales, Australia

Architect: Bourne Blue Architecture
Engineer: Izaat
Completion year: 2011
Materials: fibre cement, wood, glass panels

This exciting modern residence is located next to Diamond Beach on the mid north coast of New South Wales. On a flat site with modest views over wetlands, the house itself, rather than a stunning view, became the project's central feature — and how well this striking house deserves that prominence. A beautiful central court is warmly embraced by four unique components, each of which has an individual roofed deck, housing hammocks inviting relaxation, a dining space or the entry. Simple sliding screens close off the decks at the edge of the building, providing security and welcome protection against harsh sunlight and strong winds. This dazzling dwelling would surely be an idyllic place in which to live.

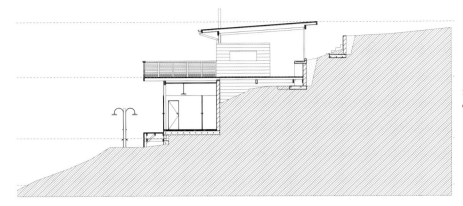

from above to below: section, living room opens up to cantilevered terrace

from above to below: view from beachside, living room

from above to below, from left to right: interior, side view,
wooden lattice façade

from above to below: bedroom, bathroom, floor plans

from left to right: view from driveway, entry staircase

general view

Point Perry Beach House

Queensland, Australia

Architect: Owen and Vokes and
Peters
Completion: 2009
Materials: stone, concrete,
wood, glass
The Point Perry Beach House project comprised an extension to an existing 1990s beach house, which was to include additional bedrooms, bathrooms and car accommodation. A promenade through this shaded site, dominated by dense coastal vegetation, reveals the fascinating nuances of setting and topography, nuances that have been subtly manipulated to establish new connections between interior and exterior elements. Masonry elements manage levels across the site, generating new and dynamic landscape spaces and anchoring the lightweight building to the terrain. Within the extension, an internal veranda provides access to bedrooms and bathrooms, resolving beautifully in a daybed nestled into the fringe of the remnant vegetation.

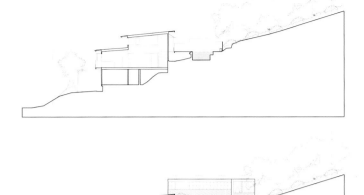

from above to below, from left to right: sections, front façade,
staircase shaft

from above to below, from left to right: view to ocean from
staircase shaft, corridor, kitchen/dining room

from above to below: exterior view from pool, interior view
from garden

from above to below: house steps down to the beach, view to terrace from dining room, floor plans

kitchen opens up to deck

exterior view

Tea Tree Beach House

Sorrento, Australia

Architect: Marcus O'Reilly
Architects
Completion year: 2008
Materials: stone, wood,
polycarbonate, glass

This low-key, site responsive, timber-clad beach house in Sorrento reinterprets a longstanding beach house tradition in the area, using local materials to blend into, pay homage to and complement its location adjacent to a national park. Floating green stained cedar volumes and bleached timbers respond visually to the eucalyptus trees that populate the site, while the rolling sand dunes remain virtually undisturbed as the volumes are structured carefully around them. A low maintenance material palette was chosen both to stand the test of riotous family life and to improve with age. Light is cleverly filtered into the interior through tea tree stake sunshades and screens, which add to the playful and unpretentious vernacular of the house.

from above to below, from left to right: hallway with skylight,
detail façade, staircase with galvanized balustrades

from above to below: interior view from deck at night, floor plan

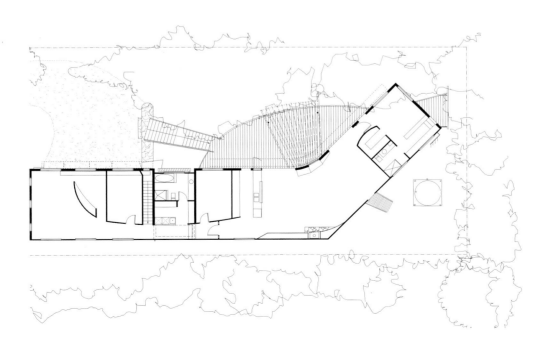

from left to right: kitchen, living room

exterior view from planted garden

Tree House

Separation Creek, Victoria, Australia

Architect: Jackson Clements Burrows
Landscape design: Ocean Road Landscaping
Completion year: 2009
Materials: cement sheet panels (painted in green tones), wood, glass

Sited in the bush fringe of Separation Creek Victoria, the project is perched on a sloping forested hillside. The steepness of the site, combined with landscape controls and landslip potential led the architects to explore a sensitive yet sculptural response that minimized the footprint by ambitiously and spectacularly echoing the form of a tree with branches. The design also draws on the modest local vernacular of 1950s painted fibro shacks with cement sheet lining. The sculptural form and associated color scheme allow the built form to both connect with the landscape and to dissolve within it. Rooms branch and cantilever in all directions from the central trunk, taking full advantage of multiple access points and stunning views.

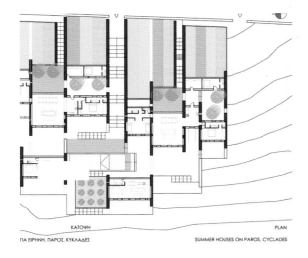

ΚΑΤΟΨΗ   PLAN

ΓΙΑ ΕΙΡΗΝΗ, ΠΑΡΟΣ, ΚΥΚΛΑΔΕΣ   SUMMER HOUSES ON PAROS, CYCLADES

from above to below: floor plans, bathroom with ocean view

from above to below: deck cantilevers out to the ocean,
house perched on a steep forested hillside above the ocean

from above to below: general view, landscape controls the
footprint of the house

from above to below: garden, interior, section

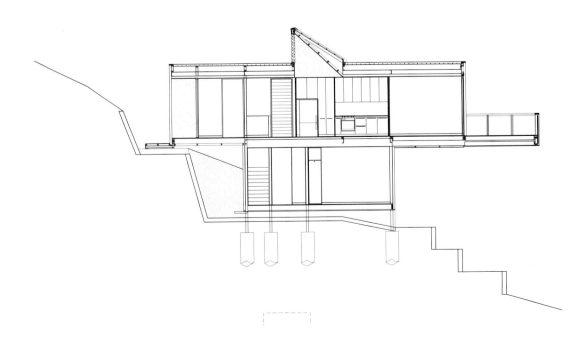

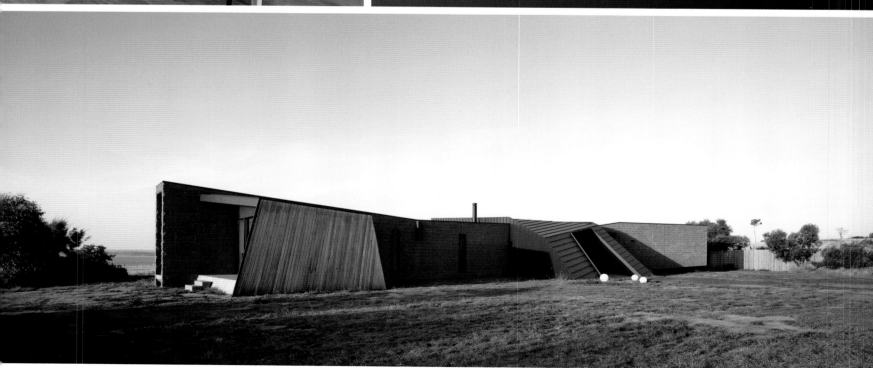

from above to below: living room, dining room, general view

exterior view from pool

Beached House

Victoria, Australia

Architect: BKK Architects
Completion year: 2010
Materials: wood, glass

With its fascinating angles and surprising projections, Beached House triumphantly claims its place as part of the beach environment, emerging from the earth as a welcome habitable dwelling in an inhospitable landscape. Inspired by the Japanese paper art of origami, the architects created a visually exciting residence that appears to unfold and refold in front of the visitor's eye in a series of subtly shifting spaces. Every internal space is directed towards the ocean and boasts a stunning marine view. It is easy to imagine that this house, dominated by wood, has been washed ashore and then "beached", embedded in the terrain, a creation of nature resting humbly within the natural world.

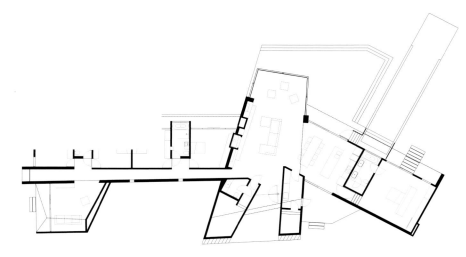

from above to below: floor plan, roof reaches down to garden

from above to below: side view, bathroom opens up to lap pool

from above to below: living room with ocean views, view from
garden

from above to below: interior structural walls, section

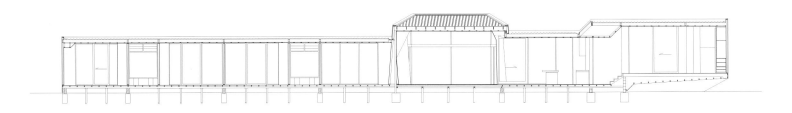

from above to below, from left to right: wooden deck, kitchen,
main entrance

exterior view from garden

Whale Beach House

Whale Beach, Australia

Architect: ARQEON
Architecture
Completion year: 2010
Materials: sandstone block,
wood, stone, glass, PV solar
panels

Whale Beach House is located in Whale Beach, Australia. The entry level floor comprises living, dining, and kitchen areas. The southern corridor well provides cross flow ventilation, stair connections, and internal natural calming light from the ceiling. The terrace of the main bedroom, which is on the top floor, is punctured to allow light to penetrate to the deck below. Although the building rises three stories, the dramatic cantilever of the top two floors allows the mass of the building to appear to hover above the ground. This in turn provides shade for the pool and entertaining area on the ground floor. The entire massing is clad in black recycled timber and forms a U-shaped black structure to the street with a floating that allows views to the horizon.

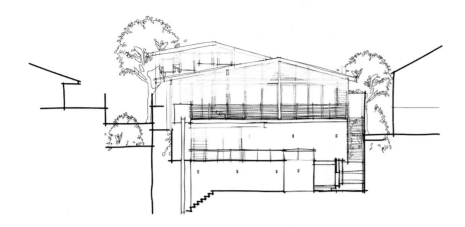

from above to below, from left to right: section, interior staircase, dining room

from above to below: exterior view, interior and exterior
become one

from above to below: living room with ocean views, garden

from above to below, from left to right: bathroom, view to
outdoor dining area, wooden staircase, elevation

Architects'/Designers' Index

01ARQ   >> 34

Los Españoles 2655
Providencia, Región Metropolitana
(Chile)
T +56.2.4929320
info@01arq.cl
www.01arq.cl

Kazuhiko Kishimoto / acaa   >> 154

4-15-40-403 Nakakaigan
Chigasaki Kanagawa
253-0055 (Japan)
T +81.467.572232
F +81.467.572129
kishimoto@ac-aa.com
www.ac-aa.com

AGi architects   >> 126, 132

38 1 Planta, Alberto Aguilera
28015 Madrid (Spain)
T +34.91.5919226
F +34.91.591922
info@agi-architects.com
www.agi-architects.com

Archipelago Design Works   >> 146

252 Senator Gil Puyat Avenue
Makati City 1200 (Philippines)
T +63.2.8866297
F +63.2.8866297
info@archipelago.ph
www.archipelago.ph

ARQEON Architecture   >> 216

Level 12, 1 Pacific Highway
North Sydney, NSW 2060
(Australia)
T +61.2.99591022
F +61.2.83246411
contact@arqeonarchitecture.com
www.arqeonarchitecture.com

Andrew Simpson Architects   >> 178

10 Bond Street
Abbotsford, Victoria 3067
(Australia)
T +61.3.94283929
mail@asimpson.com.au
www.asimpson.com.au

BKK Architects   >> 210

Level 9, 180 Russell Street
Melbourne, Victoria 3000
(Australia)
T +61.3.96714555
office@b-k-k.com.au
www.b-k-k.com.au

Bossley Architects   >> 166

2/55 Mackelvie St, Ponsonby
Auckland 1021 (New Zealand)
T +64.9.3612201
F +64.9.3612202
mail@bossleyarchitects.co.nz
www.bossleyarchitects.co.nz

Bourne Blue Architecture   >> 188

P.O. Box 295
New Castle, NSW 2300
(Australia)
T +61.2.4929.1450
F +61.2.49271623
shane@bourneblue.com.au
www.bourneblue.com.au

Alan Chu & Cristiano Kato   >> 54

Rua República Dominicana
327 - Morumbi
São Paulo, 05691-030
(Brazil)
T +55.11.981812591
projeto@escritorio.arq.br
www.chuekato.arq.br

Claesson Koivisto Rune   >> 120

Östgötagatan 50
116 64 Stockholm (Sweden)
T +46.8.6445863
F +46.8.6445883
all@ckr.se
www.claessonkoivistorune.se

Susana Cots Estudi de disseny   >> 76

Barcelona (Spain)
T +34.902.760084
info@susannacots.com
www.susannacots.com

Craig Steely Architecture   >> 62

8 Beaver Street
San Francisco, CA 94114 (USA)
T +1.415.8647013
info@craigsteely.com
www.craigsteely.com

Renato D'ettorre Architects   >> 182

19A Boundary Street
Rushcutters Bay, NSW 2011
(Australia)
T +61.2.93321061
F +61.2.93321071
info@dettorrearchitects.com.au
www.dettorrearchitects.com.au

elton+léniz Arquitectos Asociados   >> 40

Hernán Pietro Vial 1738
Vitacura, Santiago (Chile)
T +56.2.7897513
contacto@eltonleniz.cl
www.eltonleniz.cl

**Atelier d'Architecture
Bruno Erpicum & Partners**   >> 82

Avenue Baron Albert d'Huart 331
Crainhem 1950 (Belgium)
T +32.2.6872717
F +32.2.6875680
aabe@aabe.be
www.erpicum.org

graciastudio / Jorge Gracia   >> 58

651 Progressive Avenue
Suite #200
San Diego, CA, 92154 (USA)
T +1.619.7957864
info@graciastudio.com
www.graciastudio.com

Gabriel Grinspum + Mariana Simas   >> 50

Alameda Tiête
505 – Cerqueira César
São Paulo, SP 01417-020 (Brazil)
T +55.1130813522
info@marciokogan.com.br
www.marciokogan.com.br

Herbst Architects   >> 158

9/116 St Georges Bay Rd Parnell
Auckland 1052 (New Zealand)
T +64.9.3779106
F +64.9.3779103
lance@herbstarchitects.co.nz
www.herbstarchitects.co.nz

**Huttunen–Lipasti–Pakkanen
Architects**   >> 110

Iso Roobertinkatu 41
00120 Helsinki (Finland)
T +358.9.6947724
mail@h-l-p.fi
www.h-l-p.fi

Jackson Clements Burrows   >> 204

One Harwood Place
Melbourne, VIC 3000 (Australia)
T +61.3.96546227
F +61.3.96546195
jacksonclementsburrows
@jcba.com.au
www.jcba.com.au

Juma Architects   >> 96

Biezekapelstraat 1c
9000 Gent (Belgium)
T +32.479.875079
contact@jumaarchitects.com
www.jumaarchitects.com

Kerr Ritchie Architects   >> 162

PO Box 1894
Queenstown 9438 (New Zealand)
T +64.3.4414513
info@kerrritchie.com
www.kerrritchie.com

Magma   >> 92

Carrer de Bailen, 22
08010 Barcelona (Spain)
T +34.93.3010305
info@magmaarquitectura.com
www.magmaarquitectura.com

marià castelló, arquitecte   >> 88

Es Pujol de s'Era, Apartat de
Correus 130, Cami Vell de la Mola
2,3, 07860 Formentera (Spain)
T +34.97.1328046
mcastello@m-ar.net
www.m-ar.net

Marcus O'Reilly Architects   >> 200

19 Baker Street
St Kilda, VIC 3182 (Australia)
T +61.3.95343715
marcus@marcusoreilly.com
www.marcusoreilly.com

Estudio Martin Gomez Arquitectos   >> 8, 12

Ruta 10, Km 161, La Barra
Punta del Este (Uruguay)
T +598.42.772004
gomezarq@adinet.com.uy
www.martingomezarquitectos.com

MU Architecture   >> 66, 72

4529 Rue Clark
Montreal, QC H2T 2R3 (Canada)
T +1.514.9079092
F +1.514.5293033
info@architecture-mu.com
www.architecture-mu.com

Owen and Vokes and Peters   >> 194

PO Box 3917
South Brisbane Q4101
(Australia)
T +61.7.38462044
F +61.7.38466200
mail@owenandvokesandpeters.com
www.owenandvokesandpeters.com

Panorama   >> 44

San Patricio 4150
Vitacura, Santiago (Chile)
T +56.9.90373281
panorama@panorama
arquitectos.com
www.panoramaarquitectos.com

React Architects
>> 106

Samou 7A
Dionisos 145 69 (Greece)
T +30.210.8061277
F +30.210.8061282
info@re-act.gr
www.re-act.gr

Redgen Mathieson
>> 172

102/16-28 Foster St Surry Hills
NSW 2010 (Australia)
T +61.2.92804100
info@redgenmathieson.com
www.redgenmathieson.com

Reiulf Ramstad Arkitekter
>> 116

Øvregate 7
0551 Oslo (Norway)
T +47.22.808480
F +47.22.808481
firma@rra.no
www.rra.no

riofrio+rodrigo arquitectos
>> 18

Victor Maurtua 140
Lima 15073 (Peru)
T +51.1.2222572
contacto@rrmr.com.pe
www.rrmr.com.pe

Saenz de Santamaria Designs
>> 138

P.O Box 70
Koh Tao, Surat Thani 84360
(Thailand)
T +66.856556523
stay@kohtaocasas.com
www.kohtaocasas.com

Taller 33 ARQ / Martín Dulanto
>> 26

Calle Tejada 514 Interior A
Miraflores, Lima (Peru)
T +511.4455614
mds@t33arq.com
www.t33arq.com

Tierra Design
>> 142

42/145 Stirling Highway
Nedlands, WA 6009 (Australia)
T +61.8.93897933
F +61.8.93897922
perth@tierradesign.com
www.tierradesign.com

Vértice Arquitectos
>> 22, 30

Avenida 28 de Julio
Miraflores 15074 (Peru)
T + 51.1.2421131
info@verticearquitectos.com
www.verticearquitectos.com

WMR Arquitectos
>> 44

Espoz 4066
Vitacura, Región Metropolitana,
(Chile)
T +56.9.7442439
info@wmrarq.cl
www.wmrarq.cl

Xavier Vendrell Studio
>> 102

2618 N. Francisco
Chicago, IL 60647 (USA)
T +1. 773.3420085
x@xaviervendrellstudio.com
www.xaviervendrellstudio.com

Yamamori Architect & Associates
>> 150

2-1-25 Uehonmachinishi Chuo-ku
542-0062 Osaka (Japan)
T +81.6.67615596
T +816.67615596
ty@y-architect.com
www.y-architect.com

Picture Credits

Cover: Francesca Giovanelli
Backcover from above to below, from left to right:
Mauricio Fuertes Photography, John Gollings,
Mauricio Fuertes Photography

All other pictures were made available by the architects or designers.